A Moose for Jessica

text by Pat A. Wakefield with Larry Carrara

photographs by Larry Carrara

A Puffin Unicorn

A few of the photographs in this book
were graciously provided by
friends and relatives of Larry Carrara.

Pat A. Wakefield and Larry Carrara
would like to thank Eleanor and Charles Siple
for the kind permission to quote from their letter to
the Carraras on the second-to-last page of this book.

Unicorn is a registered trademark of Dutton Children's Books.

Library of Congress number 87-13663
ISBN 0-14-036134-0

Published in the United States by Dutton Children's Books,
a division of Penguin Books USA Inc.
375 Hudson Street, New York, New York 10014

Designer: Alice Lee Groton

Printed in the U.S.A.
First Unicorn Edition 1992
10 9 8 7 6 5 4 3 2

to Shawna and Adam
P.A.W.

to Bennie and Elizabeth Carrara
L.C.

It began with Ike, the dog, barking.

Larry Carrara and his wife, Lila, were having breakfast early that Saturday morning when Ike set up a fearful racket outdoors. The cows joined in, bellowing.

"What on earth is going on?" asked Lila.

Larry excused himself and went to see.

He stood on the front porch and gazed out at the late October country-side. His farm, called Carrara's Mountain, sits high in the hills of Shrews-bury, Vermont. The main road cuts through his property, only fifteen feet from the old colonial farmhouse.

Across the road, three of his cows were grazing in a pasture bordering twenty or so acres of heavily wooded land. Things looked all right there. He glanced at the cattle in the pasture next to his house. Nothing strange there, either. Larry went back inside.

The bellowing and barking resumed, however, so he got up again. Now the cows across the road were mooing loudly, staring into the woods. Larry scanned the stand of trees at the far side of the pasture. This time he saw something—over in the low bushes at the woods' edge. "What the...? The branches are rotating like radar antennas," he said to himself.

A few seconds later, it dawned on him. Antlers.

At first he thought a deer was in the bushes. But when the antlers emerged and Larry saw the size of the body that followed, he knew differently. He shouted to Lila, "Quick! Come outside! You'll never believe it. There's a moose on our property. Hurry up before he runs away!"

Lila had never seen a moose. Most people have never seen a moose—even people who live in the mountains of Vermont. Moose are wild and solitary, and usually stay deep in the woods. So Lila was very excited as she ran to join Larry.

Larry had crossed the road for a closer look. The moose's shape and coloring provided effective camouflage. Its slender, silvery legs blended in with the tree trunks and brush, and its brownish black body faded into the dark shadows behind the trees. Its forked antlers could easily be mistaken for branches.

Larry had seen moose before, in Maine while deer hunting. And in the spring, in a far meadow where he fed his horses, he had seen a moose in Vermont for the first time. He had spotted it way off at the end of a pond, and with his binoculars he'd been able to tell that the moose's antlers were only "clubs" about ten inches long, just beginning to form. The moose had stayed only a few minutes before disappearing into the trees.

Now Larry was not more than twenty feet from a moose, and he was amazed at its size. He guessed it must be at least six feet tall from ground to shoulders, with antlers towering like a crown two feet above its huge head.

Lila crept up beside Larry, and they edged closer to the fence between the cow pasture and the woods. The moose didn't seem to notice them. It kept browsing on the branches of the balsam tree—pulling twigs into its mouth with its strong, fleshy upper lip; stripping the bark with its teeth; collecting the pieces with its lips; swallowing rapidly while still chewing.

As the moose stretched its neck to reach the higher branches, Lila whispered, "He's so big. He's the most beautiful thing I've ever seen in Shrewsbury, really. Look how he carries his antlers so proud."

Larry was studying the antlers. He knew that female moose do not grow antlers, and that males grow a new set every year. Each April the antlers start out as velvety knobs, and over the summer they lengthen and branch out. The velvet is really a soft skin, rich in blood vessels that supply calcium and other minerals to the rapidly growing, bony tissue. Antlers are actually bone. In the fall they become hard, and the velvet dries and peels off.

As Larry watched, he remembered the moose he'd seen in the spring and wondered if this were the same one, his antlers now full-grown.

The antlers were magnificent. They looked like huge, long-fingered hands, turned palms up. When the moose glanced toward Larry and Lila, Larry noticed the left one had a prong, or "finger," that curved down instead of up. He thought it might have been injured while the antler was still soft and forming.

By now Ike had stopped barking, and the cows were grazing peacefully. The moose continued to browse, periodically glancing toward the cows. If they saw him, they seemed undisturbed.

Larry and Lila watched for about half an hour, thrilled to have a moose on their property. And since it seemed that the moose wasn't about to run off, they slipped away quietly, trying not to startle him.

In the house, Larry hurriedly looked for his camera while Lila telephoned their children, their minister, and Larry's cousin. "Come on up here, we have a moose out here," she told them excitedly. She also warned them to be quiet as they arrived. Then she and Larry went back outside with the camera.

One after another, the visitors joined Larry and Lila along the fence by the woods, making themselves as inconspicuous as possible. A few times the moose looked their way, then withdrew into the brush.

Moose are unpredictable creatures and can move with surprising speed. When provoked, they may charge. So the observers stood back a nervous twenty yards, taking pictures but not crossing the fence.

They watched for hours. The moose just kept browsing, moving slowly from balsam to red maple to willow.

Larry was pretty sure that, like his cattle, moose are ruminants, animals that have stomachs with four chambers. They eat only plants, coarse fibrous food, and swallow rapidly without much chewing. The food enters the first chamber, which is like a big storage tank. When that chamber is full, the animal stops eating and finds a quiet place to rest. Then it returns small amounts of the pulpy food mass to its mouth and rechews it. The pulp is called a cud. After the cud has been thoroughly chewed, it is swallowed again and passes on to the second, third, and fourth chambers to be fully digested.

Twice while they watched, the moose lay down for about half an hour to chew his cud. Then he got up and browsed again. Finally, late in the afternoon, he stopped browsing, walked back along the fence, and disappeared into the woods.

Soon he reappeared on the other side of the fence, walking down the old logging road that led from the woods into the pasture where the three cows were grazing.

As the moose entered the pasture, one cow and a yearling calf took off like a shot and jumped the electric wire fence. The third cow, Jessica, a pudgy brown and white Hereford with a freckled nose, stood her ground and kept a wary eye on the unlikely visitor.

Larry rounded up the two cows and let them into the pasture next to the house with the rest of the herd. Then he went to the pasture across the road and joined Lila and the others. They had prudently switched to the woods side of the fence, now that the moose was on the pasture side.

The moose walked around Jessica in tighter and tighter circles. Whenever he came within a few feet of her, she would demurely step away. It seemed to Larry that she was thinking, "Look at that tall, dark, handsome fellow. So majestic and proud." At least those were Larry's thoughts. He was impressed by the noble animal.

As the sun began to set, Larry and Lila realized they had been watching the moose all day. They were tired, cold, and hungry, and it was getting hard to see. Their visitors had already left, so they went inside to warm up and to fix dinner. As they looked back into the pasture, the silhouettes of the moose and Jessica stood out against the dusky light. He was still following her around, trying to get close to her.

That night, as Lila and Larry went to bed, they talked about how lucky they felt. They could hardly believe that the moose had stayed all day. They were sure he would be gone by morning.

When Larry woke up, the first thing he did was look out the window. He could see Jessica standing by a small shed in the pasture across the road, but he didn't see the moose.

He got dressed and went outside to do his chores, which included bringing Jessica some grain in a pail. When she finished eating, he picked up the pail and rounded the shed. Much to his surprise, there was the moose, five feet away. Larry slowly put the pail down and stepped back. The moose came forward, sniffed the pail curiously, then walked off.

The moose stayed with Jessica, following her around just as he had the first day. By late morning she let him get close enough to nuzzle her. And when she ate, he'd rest his neck on her back and move his head back and forth in a gentle caress.

Larry and Lila watched them all morning. By afternoon they realized they now had two days of chores to catch up on, so they reluctantly got down to business, sneaking a look whenever they could.

Later in the day, as Larry went to put hay in the shed for Jessica, he got a feeling…a feeling that someone or something was close by, watching him.

He turned around. The moose was just a few feet away. He had appeared without a sound. "Oh brother," thought Larry. "What's going to happen now?" He was afraid an abrupt movement would startle the moose into charging. So he slowly continued putting hay in the shed. The moose observed him a few seconds more (to Larry it seemed like hours), and then walked off and joined Jessica on the other side of the pasture.

The rest of the day, whenever Larry or Lila looked, the moose was either beside Jessica or back in the woods browsing. Occasionally he tried to mount her. Once, the moose was lying down about five feet from where Jessica was resting. They were slowly chewing their cuds, staring into each other's eyes.

After dinner, Larry crossed the road and the moose came to the fence. Larry said, "Hi, big fellow. You sure surprised us by staying another day." He realized he could reach right out and touch the moose. But he thought to himself, "He's a wild animal, and I shouldn't try to encourage him or do anything to domesticate him." He remembered stories he'd read that when you touch a wild animal you are taking that wildness away, so he decided he would not touch the moose.

That evening Larry phoned the State Game Warden, Don Gallus, from nearby Mount Holly. He told him about the moose and asked him to have a look in the morning if the moose were still there. Larry wanted assurance that the moose was healthy and safe, and that he wouldn't harm his animals or anyone else.

The next morning, Monday, Larry did his chores before going to work. When he saw that the moose was still with Jessica, he called Mr. Gallus. Then he decided that when he got to work, he would explain about the moose and arrange to take some time off, perhaps until the moose left. He wasn't sure what might happen, but he thought he should be home just in case.

Lila was nervous after Larry left. She was afraid the moose might leave while he was gone, and she didn't like being the only one home, peeking outside every now and then to see if the moose were still there. She was relieved when Mr. Gallus drove up, and she walked with him out to the pasture.

Mr. Gallus was surprised to see a moose so at home with a cow. He explained to Lila that cows are members of the Bovidae family, which includes buffalo and sheep, while moose are members of the Cervidae, or deer family, which includes caribou, white-tailed deer, and elk. Moose are the largest antlered animals in the world. Young bulls grow their first set of antlers when they are about a year old, and each subsequent year the new set of antlers is larger and more filled in, or palmate. He estimated that this moose weighed about seven hundred pounds and, judging by his size and the size of his antlers, was about two-and-a-half years old.

Lila went back into the house, and Mr. Gallus watched the moose. He wanted to see if the moose showed any signs of brainworm, a disease moose sometimes get from ingesting the egg cases of a parasite whose normal host is the white-tailed deer. In a moose, the parasite larvae develop, move through the bloodstream to the spinal cord, and eventually migrate to the brain where they feed on brain tissue. In addition to affecting eyesight, movement, and breathing, brainworm will cause a moose to sway and lose its balance whenever it tries to stand in one position for long. It also seems to lose its fear of man. So Mr. Gallus observed this moose closely.

Around noon, Larry came home and told Lila he had arranged for a leave of absence from his job. Then he joined Mr. Gallus, who reported that the moose appeared to be in good health, even though it was unusual for one to let people get so close.

Larry asked Mr. Gallus where he thought the moose had come from.

"We estimate that eight to twelve moose live in the mountains within a thirty-five mile radius of your farm," he told him. "I know that Charles Willey, head of Vermont's Moose Project, estimates that there are probably only three hundred to six hundred moose in all of Vermont. Since they're normally solitary animals and don't travel in herds, it's difficult to say exactly how many there are."

He explained that fall is the moose breeding, or rutting, season. Male

moose have a strong instinct to breed, and they sometimes engage in shoving matches with other males, using their antlers and pawing the ground with their forefeet. The stronger moose may not win the female's attention, however, because apparently it is the female moose, called a moose cow, that chooses to accept the male.

Mr. Gallus surmised that this moose hadn't been able to find a willing moose cow where he lived, so he wandered out of the deep woods and ended up on Carrara's Mountain. When he saw Jessica and she didn't run away, the moose decided to stay. He had found his cow, never mind that she was a Hereford cow, not another moose. Mr. Gallus laughed. "We know that moose have excellent hearing and a very good sense of smell. We also know their vision is poor. I guess this proves it."

Mr. Gallus expected that the moose would stay about ten days and then head back to wherever he had come from. A bull moose usually stays with a receptive female about ten days and then leaves to find another moose cow to mate with before his rutting period ends. Bull moose may be in rut for about two months.

After the rutting period, the antlers no longer have value for display and defense. Moose normally shed them in early to mid winter. During cold, snowy weather, moose may actually be able to forage more easily without them.

Bull moose are usually aggressive during their rutting season and do not like anyone or anything to come near their cows. Mr. Gallus wanted to be sure this moose was not dangerous.

After watching the moose for several more hours, Mr. Gallus told Larry he saw no need to tranquilize the moose to move him. He didn't appear to be dangerous and seemed quite content where he was. Mr. Gallus also thought that Larry was treating the moose kindly, not fencing him in or bothering him. There was no fence in the woods at the back of the property, and the pasture fence was only an electric wire eighteen inches off the ground. The moose's long legs, evolved for standing in deep water or snow, could easily carry him over.

Mr. Gallus promised to check on the moose again and answer questions. He left thinking that the moose would be gone in a week or so.

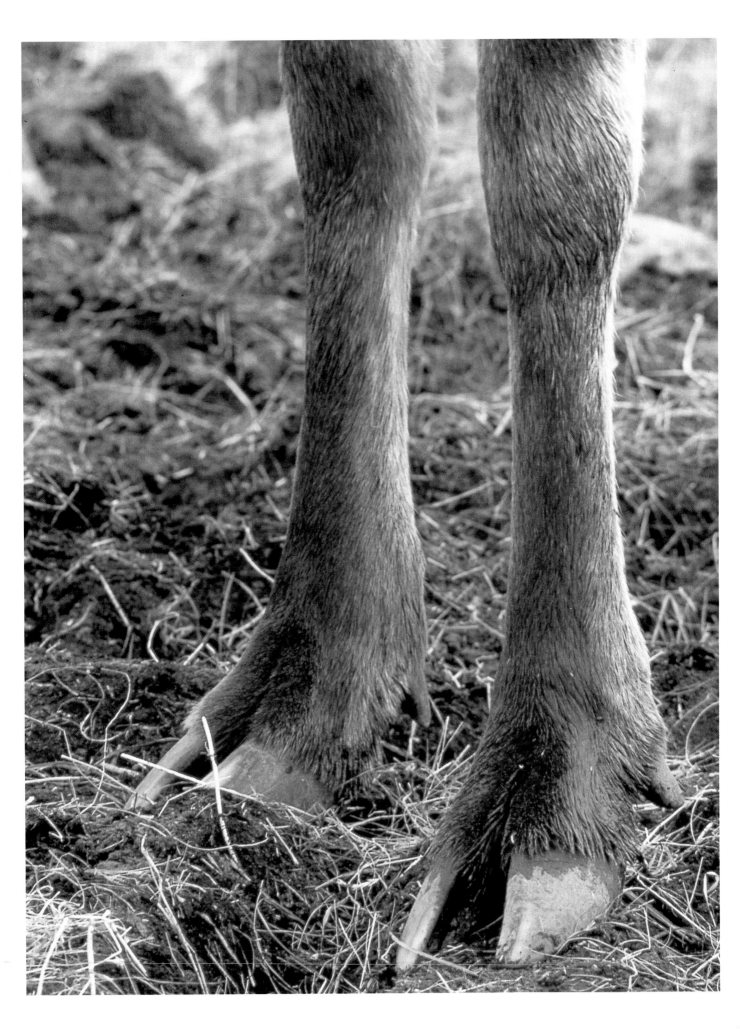

Every day from then on "was like a new thing," according to Larry. "I'd get up early and look out and say, 'Is he there?' And Lila would say no. Then by the time I'd get coffee and all, I'd look out the window and say, 'Here he comes.'" Some days the moose was in the woods browsing, his antlered head reaching high in the branches for food. Other days he'd be in the pasture, nosing after Jessica.

Larry's geese, who wandered wherever they pleased, liked to tease the moose. Sometimes when he was lying down chewing his cud, they would rush at him, flapping their wings and honking loudly. When they became too big a nuisance, he'd get up and chase them away.

Larry kept the rest of his herd in the pasture next to the house, and he no longer let Ike run free. Ike was trained to herd cattle, and he often chased Larry's horses, too. Larry knew "darn well" the dog would chase the moose, and he didn't want the moose to turn on Ike with his sharp hooves.

In the evenings Larry would go to the pasture, and the moose would come over to the fence and stretch his neck out. "How or why did you pick us?" Larry would ask him softly. "I'm glad you're here and that you're healthy, even if we can't explain your actions."

Larry watched the moose every day and got to know his routine. After browsing early in the morning, he would follow Jessica around. When she tired of him, she would seek solitude under a pine tree with branches so

low that the moose couldn't follow without tangling his antlers. He would content himself with standing a few feet away, gazing longingly at her while waiting for her to come out. Sometimes when she came out, she would go right over to him.

Larry knew that despite their behavior, the moose and Jessica could not produce offspring. Charles Willey had explained that the chromosomes of a moose and a Hereford cow do not match up.

The moose had a favorite spot to drink from in the pasture. He found a small shallow pool fed by an underground spring. To get his mouth to the water, he had to kneel down on his long front legs. Sometimes after a snowfall, instead of drinking from the spring, he would eat snow.

Nearly every day the moose found a low bush or shrub, and hooked and rubbed his antlers on it. It is what moose do in the fall, to help scrape the dried velvet off. Now this shadowboxing developed strength in the moose's neck and shoulder muscles that he could use to combat rivals.

Larry noticed that the moose urinated two or three times a day at a certain place at the edge of the woods. It seemed to Larry that he went through a ritual of sorts. After he urinated, he knelt down on his front legs and put his face over the area, not touching it, but close enough to take in his own musk, or aroma. Then he stood and threw his head back as far as his antlers would allow. Most days he did this silently. But a few times when he threw his head back, he made a loud, bugle-like noise.

Sometimes during the day he made blowing, snorting noises. His large upper lip would puff out, his nostrils would flare, and he'd expel a blast of air, vibrating his lips as he did so. The only other noises Larry ever heard him make were in the early morning and late evening, when Larry would go to the fence and the moose would come to him. Larry would talk quietly, and the moose would breathe heavily, making soft blowing sounds.

Larry gave him a private name and used it when they talked. "Thank you for coming back, Josh," Larry told him each morning. "I'm so glad to see you again. And when you leave, if you ever pass this way again, even for a moment, please give me some kind of sign or whatever, so I know it's you."

Larry had chosen the name Josh because it was the name of one of his grandsons. And it sounded like the word he used when he called his cows. If he slipped and said "Josh" when others were around, he could always claim, "I was just saying 'Boss, come Boss,' talking to the cows."

Larry knew that once the moose shed his antlers, it would be very difficult to tell him apart from other moose. He had noticed one other distinctive marking, however. The moose had a small V-shaped scar above his right eye. Larry thought the moose might have cut himself earlier in the year, perhaps running through the woods, or during the accident or fight that damaged his antler. He hoped that as the moose matured, the scar would stay visible.

Ten days passed, then twenty, and the moose was still there. Word of his visit spread. Newspapers, magazines, radio and television stations sent reporters to cover the story. Mr. Gallus dropped by several more times, and busloads of schoolchildren, local people, and others who had heard or read about the moose came to see for themselves. Some arrived as early as six in the morning. Others drove up after dark and shined their headlights into the pasture. Everyone found it unusual and funny and even a little touching that a wild moose had come to court a farmer's cow. They called them The Odd Couple, and called him The Lovesick Moose and The Shrewsbury Moose.

Some people suggested that Larry put up a wooden fence and charge admission. He did exactly the opposite. He cut down the wire at the back of the pasture bordering the woods and turned off the electricity in the rest of the fence. He wanted to be absolutely sure the moose could leave whenever he wished.

Other people told Lila she should set up a food concession and sell hot dogs and coffee. Some even wanted to sell their own wares. To all, Larry and Lila's answer was a firm no. "I don't want any vendors around. I've kept all vendors out," said Larry to a visitor. "I don't want to make it a sideshow here." Larry did respond to requests for souvenirs, however, by having T-shirts, bumper stickers, and other small mementos made up.

Larry was glad he'd arranged for a leave of absence from his job. He needed to be home to help Lila with the crowds and to make sure people didn't try to get into the pasture and startle the moose.

One day Larry had to return to the house for a moment, leaving a crowd watching the moose. He told them, "Please, and I mean *please,* don't go near the moose." But by the time he headed back, the eager visitors had pressed forward, almost trapping the moose in the brush. The moose charged. "We had three hundred people running in every direction," said Larry. "I ran up as quickly as possible, but there was this young girl, and he was running right toward her. I hollered, and for some reason the moose stopped, not but two or three feet from her. I don't know why, but he did. No one was hurt, and everything was fine after that."

Sometimes the moose would be lying down when people came, and they'd say to Larry, "Gee, I've been here for a while. Doesn't he ever get up?"

And Larry would say, "Oh, yes. But if he's resting, I don't harass him and say, 'Hurry and get up so people can see you.'"

If the moose had been lying down a few hours and people did wait, then Larry might go inside the fence and say, "Come on, get up. People want to see you." And when the moose would stand up, people would be amazed at how big he was.

Deer hunting season would start November 15, and Larry and Mr. Gallus worried about the moose's safety, even though it's against the law to shoot a moose in Vermont. They hoped he'd stay on Larry's farm until the season was over and not return to the forest where a hunter might mistake him for a deer. Larry posted No Hunting signs on his property near the house and back into the woods, to help protect the moose.

On the first day of the deer hunting season, the twenty-second day of the moose's visit, Larry got up at six thirty and went outside to look for him. He didn't see him with Jessica, and he couldn't find him in the woods. Larry was afraid he'd left for good. Even though he had known that the moose would leave sometime, he felt a keen sense of loss.

It was chilly outside, so Larry went into the house for warmer clothes. In his back bedroom, he happened to glance out the window into the pasture by the house, and there, much to his surprise, was the moose! Even more surprising, the other cattle were there too.

As Larry watched, the moose started toward the cattle, and they trotted off to another part of the pasture. The moose tried several times to approach them, sometimes running directly at them, but they'd always dash away.

That was the first time the moose had crossed the road and entered the pasture next to the house. Until then, he'd stayed across the road with Jessica day and night. Larry wondered where Jessica was now. He went outside and saw that she was still in the pasture on the other side of the road, looking toward the house. Larry couldn't tell whether she could see the moose or not.

Late in the afternoon, the moose finally gave up trying to get near the cattle and lay down near the fence by the road. Larry noticed that the moose wasn't chewing his cud as he usually did when he lay down. He was just staring across the road toward the woods and Jessica. There were no balsam trees and very few other trees in the pasture near the house, and Larry thought the moose must be hungry. So he asked the people who were milling about, watching the moose, to move their cars, stand back, and make room.

Sure enough, as soon as a space was cleared, the moose stretched his legs and stood up. Larry raised his arms to signal people to stay back. He talked gently to the moose. "Come on, big boy. You must be hungry. It's okay. Let's go." The moose stepped over the low fence, walked proudly across the road, stepped over another low fence, and joined Jessica in the pasture.

He caressed her with his head, and as she continued to eat hay, he lay down beside her. Only later did he go to the balsam trees to eat. In the evening, when Larry and Lila checked to see what was going on outside, the moose had again crossed over to the pasture by the house, leaving Jessica by herself.

The next morning when he looked outside, Larry was curious to see which pasture the moose was in, if he were around at all. Larry spotted the moose in the corner of the pasture next to the house. When he went outside to feed the animals, he was startled to find Jessica standing beside the house, staring across the fence at the moose and the other cattle in the pasture. She had evidently managed to get over the low wire fence across the road but had been stopped by this one, even though it was the same height.

Larry unhooked the gate and let her in. She walked slowly over to the moose, rubbed his shoulder with her head, and started to nibble hay that was on the ground. The moose put his head down and pushed hay toward her mouth with his nose, then rested his head on her back while she ate.

This day the other cattle didn't run away from the moose. In fact, they let him herd them up whenever they were near the feeding area. The moose would push them gently with his head, sometimes using his antlers. If they were slow to respond, he'd stomp his front feet and move toward them aggressively.

One of the young bulls, Carson, who was just four months old, seemed especially fond of the moose. Every time Larry looked, it seemed that Carson was at the moose's side or following him around. Carson was so small, he could almost walk underneath the moose.

When Larry and Lila went to bed that night, they remarked that it was the first night since the moose's arrival that all the cattle and the moose were together in the same pasture.

In the morning, Larry went about his chores as usual and talked to people who came to have a look at The Lovesick Moose and his friend Jessica. He got tired of telling people which cow was Jessica, so he tied a red ribbon around her neck.

Over the next few days, Larry noticed that the moose's routine had changed. At mid-morning and again around three in the afternoon, he would stand near the fence and look longingly across the road. Larry would clear a path through the crowd for him to cross. Once on the other side, the moose would head down the old logging road and disappear into the woods for two or three hours.

Larry believed the moose needed to widen his range, since he'd probably eaten all the nourishing shoots and twigs nearby. After browsing for a few hours, he'd cross the road again, join the cattle in the pasture, and lie down to chew his cud, gazing out over the valley.

After a heavy snowfall, Larry thought it might be tiring for the moose to plow through the deep snow. The holiday season was approaching, and Larry's nephew was selling Christmas trees. So Larry cut boughs from the trees and brought them into the pasture when he brought hay for the cattle. Sometimes during the day, the moose would lick the block of salt that Larry put out for the cattle.

In the evenings, the moose acted like the chieftain of the barnyard and herded the cattle up to the hay. Then he would maneuver himself into the

group and push hay toward Jessica, as though he wanted to make sure she got her fair share (or more). The moose never ate any of the feed put out for the cattle.

After eating, they would all lie down and chew their cuds, and the moose always lay near Jessica. Around ten at night, he'd get up and cross the road again, heading toward the woods. Sometimes he'd walk toward the far meadow, where the horses were. He always returned around seven in the morning, and Larry and Lila were always overjoyed to see him.

"Jessica looks kind of con-
fused."—Onlooker
"Everyone in love looks con-
fused."—Larry

"He's giving that guy in the brown
pants another leer." —Onlooker
"You don't have to worry until the
ears go down."—Larry

By New Year's Eve, the moose had been on Carrara's Mountain sixty-eight days. Larry and Lila had been driven by limousine to appear on nationwide television. They had been interviewed by telephone and broadcast over the radio to such far-off places as San Francisco, Australia, and Austria. Pictures, stories, and letters had appeared in newspapers and magazines around the world. People had composed poems and songs about the unusual courtship. And over seventy thousand visitors had traveled up the narrow country road to Carrara's Mountain. On one Saturday, over four thousand people visited the farm.

"A guy came yesterday with a great big tele-photo lens and everything else, you know. He's taking pictures and then he says, 'Boy, what a stupid-looking moose.' And I said, 'Well, listen, fella, how far did you drive to come up here? You came up to see him. He didn't come down to see you.' So I mean, that will probably tell you something."—Larry

"Of all the people that came, I never heard of anybody that was disappointed. They'd say, 'I never expected him to be that close and be so gentle. I can't get over how he's so close and he doesn't hurt anyone.'"—Lila

"A lot of people that come, especially the elderly, say, 'Gee, I'm eighty years old, or sixty-five years old, and never in my life had the opportunity to view a moose at this distance.' A lot of people said, 'You know, we're sick of assassinations and we're sick of politics and hostages. It came just at an opportune time, and it certainly has brought a lot of love.'"—Larry

Larry and Lila received letters from children and adults around the world. Many were addressed uniquely: *The Moose Farm, Shoesbury, Vermont* or *The Farmer and the Moose, Shrewsbury, Vermont*. A few told Larry that many years ago, moose had visited their farms in Maine or Montana. Everyone thanked Larry and Lila for being so kind to the moose.

Larry and Lila tried to prepare themselves for the end of the moose's rutting season. They knew he would shed his antlers and then probably leave. Charles Willey had told them that when moose lose their antlers, they apparently feel defenseless and retreat to the forest for the rest of the winter.

Larry's leave of absence was over on Monday, January 5. He was apprehensive about returning to work while the moose was still there. Since the moose's arrival, Larry had barely left the farm. He had always been careful to wait until the moose was settled before driving to town on errands. "I would wait until he lay down and then I would figure no one is going to harass him or anything, so I'd run downtown."

Most times when Larry got back, Lila would report, "The minute you left, he took off, and he just returned a few minutes before you did." Though it seemed strange that the moose would disappear when Larry left and reappear just before he returned, it did happen. Larry believed the moose did not feel safe when he wasn't around.

Reluctantly, Larry went back to work. Around nine thirty that morning, as Lila watched, the moose walked off into the woods, but he came back about three thirty in the afternoon, just before Larry came home.

The moose stayed with the cattle, lying down with them in the early evening. Eventually he left them and lay down right beside the house, something he had never done before. He was there when Larry went to bed. On Tuesday, his pattern was the same.

Wednesday, the moose again loped into the woods. In the late morning, Larry received a phone call at work. It was Lila and his nephew. "Can you come home? Right now? The moose is back and one antler is missing!"

Larry drove home quickly. The moose was in the pasture with the cattle, pushing hay toward them. Carson and Jessica were beside him. His head looked lopsided, with a tall, stately antler on one side, and a raw red patch on the other. Even though Larry knew the antler was supposed to come off, he thought the moose looked embarrassed, as though his pride had been diminished and he didn't feel as powerful and noble as before.

As Larry walked into the pasture to put out more hay for the cattle, the moose followed a few feet behind. Wherever Larry went, "the moose would smell the track where I was and walk right in it. I mean, usually I'd walk in his track, you know; he and I were two individuals. But this last day, he and I were together. He walked in my tracks and followed me." Larry felt that night would probably be the last night he would see the moose. He wondered, "Is he trying to say something to me…tell me, you know, this is it."

The moose was just one footstep behind him when Larry turned around. Larry wondered, "Does he want me to touch him? Or just say good-bye like I always do at night?" During their nightly conversations Larry had said things like, "There were a lot of people here today. You did this or you did that. Did you notice so and so?" Sometimes he'd say to himself, "What am I talking to a moose like this for?" But it had just seemed natural.

Throughout the moose's stay, it seemed to Larry that people would ask a million times, "Have you touched him?" And he would say, "No, I didn't touch him." And they'd ask, "Why?" Larry would reply, "Because of that bit of wildness that he has." They would say, "Look, he's a pet." Larry didn't agree. "It's obvious he does like it here, but he's still wild and he's going to stay that way." And they'd say, "Well, why don't you touch him just for the sake of being the only one to touch him?" Larry would answer, "He has become very, very fearless of everybody, and people don't seem to bother him and all that. But this last little bit of wildness that he has, I won't take it from him."

Lila had always worried that the moose would do something to hurt Larry, but Larry had told her, "I know he would never hurt me. He's had plenty of chances. There is no way in the world I'd ever harm him, and I think he knows that. Sometimes wild animals have more sense than a lot of people."

As Larry stood one footstep from the moose, he thought about their morning and evening talks and the trust that had developed between them. He didn't touch him.

That night, the moose lay down as usual with Jessica and the other cattle. Later he moved closer to the house, right by the porch. Larry tried to stay awake all night, but he dozed off. When he woke up, the moose was no longer by the porch, and Larry couldn't see him in the pasture. Before he went to work, he searched but he didn't find him. Larry left, not expecting the moose to return, yet hoping that he might.

About ten in the morning, Lila received a phone call from a neighbor who lived a mile away. The moose had passed through her barnyard that morning, heading toward Salt Ash Mountain, east of Larry's farm. Both antlers were gone, and he was trotting straight ahead, as though he knew where he was going.

So far, the moose has not returned. He stayed at Carrara's Mountain for seventy-six days. Mr. Gallus and Mr. Willey believe he spent the winter within a few miles of Larry's farm, high in the mountains. Nobody really knows whether he will return after his antlers grow back and his mating instincts grow strong again. Moose have a good sense of direction, so he should be able to find his way back if he wants to.

Nobody really knows, either, if Jessica misses him. She stays a bit apart from the rest of the cattle, but otherwise she is her usual docile self, seemingly content munching hay and chewing her cud.

Larry and Lila miss seeing the moose each morning. They miss the crowds of people, too, although they are still receiving cards and letters from all over the world, thanking them for their "kindness…toward the moose and the extension of that kindness in accepting all the visitors."

They have asked themselves many times, "Why did he come to us? Why here?" Their children supplied perhaps the best answer. "The children said we love company," Lila remarked, "so that's why he picked this house."

Larry and Lila will be looking for the moose in the fall. They wonder if his antlers will grow in again with one "finger" pointing down, and they hope that the small scar above his right eye will still be there. That way they can be sure.